THE COMPLETE GUIDE TO LONG TERM INJURY PREVENTION

THE COACHES GUIDE TO LONG TERM INJURY PREVENTION

The Complete 5 Step Process You Need to Help Your Clients Avoid Injury & Achieve Results They Didn't Believe Possible

Sarah J. Pitts

The Coaches Guide To Long Term Injury Prevention Copyright © 2021 by Sarah J. Pitts. All Rights Reserved.

All rights reserved. No part of this book may be reproduced in any form or by any electronic or mechanical means including information storage and retrieval systems, without permission in writing from the author. The only exception is by a reviewer, who may quote short excerpts in a review.

Sarah J Pitts
Visit my website at http://www.mostmotion.com

First Printing: April 2021

Dedication

For Mum, Dad and Louise, my first and best teachers in problem solving, independent thinking and never giving up.

For my partner Pete, who worked his fingers to the bone so that I could pursue my dream.

For Grandad, who always believed I'd be "driving that Bentley one day".

For Jim Edwards, who taught me how to turn my ideas into reality.

Quotes

"Bamboo that bends is stronger than oak that resists".
– Japanese Proverb

"Unity is strength... where there is collaboration, wonderful things can be achieved".
– Mattie Stepanek

CONTENTS

Introduction 1
   Here's How To Succeed With This Guide 2
   Who Is This Guide For? 3
   Here's What We're Going To Cover 6

Injury Prevention Lessons From The Dog Whisperer? 11
The Five Steps Of Injury Prevention 19
Step #1 – Breaking the Barriers 21
   1.1: Creating Deeper Connections 21
   1.2: Changing Your Language 25
   1.3: Insider Secrets 32
   1.4: The "Eyes, Ears, Ask, Give" Strategy 33
   1.5: Transforming Your communication 42
   1.6: Daily Checklist 43

Step #2: Activating Stealth Mode 45
   2.1: The Challenge: Put Your Money Where Your Mouth Is! 48
   2.2: Changing Lives Through Injury Prevention 54
   2.3: What's The Secret? 56
   2.4: How To Make Injury Prevention Easy 58

Step #3: Building Your Superpowers 61
   3.1: You Get The Best Results From Strength Training – If You Do It Right 62
   3.2: Strength + Variety = Resilience 64

- 3.3: The Results Generation Formula 65
- 3.4: Case Study: Chris Yates 67

Step #4: Connecting The Dots – Stepping Into Your Full Potential 69
- 4.1: Taking Your Coaching To The Next Level 71
- 4.2: When Connecting The Dots Fails 74
- 4.3: The Whole Human Method – 3 Converging Factors 81
- 4.4: A Unique Solution 83

Step #5: Becoming Indispensable 87
- 5.1: The Communication Network 88

Introducing The SMARTT® Methods 93
- Level 1: The Vault of Injury Prevention Secrets 95
- Level 2 The SMARTT® Coach Certification 96
- Level 3: Technique & Performance Specialist 97
- Level 4: Injury Prevention & Recovery Specialist 98
- Level 5: The Change Makers' Mastermind 99
- Bonus: The SMARTT® Safe Mark 101
- Case Study: Justine Hudson 102

Revealed! The True Power Of Injury Prevention 107
A Personal Message From Sarah J. Pitts 113

INTRODUCTION

For sports coaches, fitness coaches and personal trainers, this is **The Coaches Guide to Long-Term Injury Prevention Success** - the complete five-step process you need to help your clients avoid injury and deliver fitness results they didn't believe possible.

Right now, don't even *think* about mobility training, improving movement or trying to prevent injury. Wait until you read this guide, as I can promise you, by the end, you're going to have a different approach.

If you're doing, or getting even getting ready to do, any one of these things with your clients...STOP! Foam rolling, stretching, strength training, warming up, cooling down, programming sessions, delivering sessions, doing course after course to keep learning.

There's *nothing wrong* with these techniques. In fact, some of them are vital to the safety of your sessions, but we're going to take them and your coaching skills to the next level. Are you ready?

HERE'S HOW TO SUCCEED WITH THIS GUIDE

Welcome to the guide. The Coronavirus of 2020 changed everything for sports and fitness coaches. It showed us just how vulnerable clients are when the healthcare and other medical support networks are shut down and unable to help with their injuries.

It showed us how reliant we've become on the treatment of injuries. Not only that, but the huge opportunities available to us as coaches to not only help prevent these problems, but to stand head and shoulders above all the other coaches out there as we do it. Trust me when I say it's in your best interest to read every word of this guide, understand it and implement it.

There's over 30 years of fitness coaching, movement analysis, injury prevention and tree injury treatment speaking here. I'll tell you more about myself in a minute. But first, let's get back to **you**.

Your income relies on attendance to your sessions, and the results you can generate from them, so it's paramount that you keep your clients training consistently. But the chances are that you aren't spending much time when you're on mobility in your sessions right now. I've taught countless coaches and individuals how to blend my unique injury prevention methods into their training sessions, so they don't have to spend extra time on mobility, or try to convince clients to do it, they can simply get on with what they love.

I've created the simplest processes, systems and an approach that will do 95% of the work for you. And I can guarantee it's unlike anything you've ever seen before. You will be able to build the strategy on your own. But there are also groups training and services that can assist you as well.

WHO IS THIS GUIDE FOR?

So, who **is** this guide for? Let's make sure this guide is for you before you read any further. This guide was written specifically for parent volunteer coaches, club coaches, part time group instructors, physical education teachers, and full-time fitness professionals of all kinds. In other words, coaches who care about the welfare of their clients even after the session has ended. Coaches who love to watch their clients succeed, and coaches who love to make a difference.

These methods are **not** created for assistant coaches or newly qualified coaches. There's far too much already on your plate! You're still thinking about where you need to position yourself, what you should be teaching and making sure you give appropriate teaching points. The last thing you need is to yet more techniques to remember!

To get the very best from this guide and the techniques described, you should have a valid certification that qualifies you to run your own sessions without supervision. That means your governing body recognises you as a qualified coach within their organisation and you are confident delivering your own sessions.

You might not have any mobility or injury prevention experience yet, but that's okay. We just need to make sure the foundations are in place.

The Choice is Yours

The choice is yours, but I don't really think you have a choice. I'm from Yorkshire in the UK and Yorkshire folk have a reputation of straight talking. That's why I'm going to be straight with you.

My guess is that you are reading this guide because you're trying to figure out how you can do more to help your clients avoid injury. I don't know why you decided to do this right now, but obviously you don't have the answer you were looking for. Otherwise, you wouldn't need to explore what I have to say.

The truth is most people won't read every word in this guide. They won't take action and that won't benefit their clients. They say they're trying to help, but when it comes down to it, they don't take the actions needed to make any significant difference in their clients' lives. There are many reasons for that.

Some think it's too hard, or they don't believe they can do it. Some think they know it all, so they won't even try, and some don't consider it important enough. But the most common reason by a long way is that they think it won't work for them. And if you're one of these people, you have my permission to stop reading right now. Why? Because you've already set yourself up to fail. You are what you think.

Is it easy to prevent injuries? No, but it's not as difficult as the industry makes out either. In fact, I'm doing everything I can to simplify the process for you. I'm going to introduce you to the very best mobility strategies in the industry. Every strategy I'm about to reveal has been 100% created by me. There's nothing I stole from anyone else, and where others have inspired me, I will absolutely give credit where credit is due. All I ask is that you make a commitment right now. Be open minded, positive and have the discipline and consistency to make it through this guide. If you don't understand everything you read right now, that's okay. I'm here to help you and have a community you can join when you're done reading this. I also have coaching programmes and workshops. So, rest assured you're in great hands. Let's go.

HERE'S WHAT WE'RE GOING TO COVER

Over the next few chapters, we'll be covering what I've come to recognise as the basic principles of injury prevention. These are five steps that are crucial to the long-term success of your injury prevention efforts.

Within step one, which is breaking the barriers, we're going to cover four fundamental questions you'll need to answer before the start of every session. We'll also discuss my powerful "Eyes, Ears, Ask, Give" strategy, which I promise is like seeing into the matrix!

In step two, which is activating stealth mode, we're going to cover the biggest challenge you face as a coach...and the simple secret to successful injury prevention.

In step three, which is building your superpowers, we're going to cover your most powerful injury prevention weapon, that injury specialists and medical professionals can't even hope to harness...and my "Super Results Generation Formula", which will give you super quick (and oftentimes, surprising) results.

In step four, which is connecting the dots, we're going to look at how the industry is currently failing, what that means for you and your clients, and my "Whole Human Method", which creates a truly elegant solution.

Finally, in step five, which is becoming indispensable, we'll look at how small changes make big differences and the true power of injury prevention. And then at the end, there's a personal note from me.

By now, you might be wondering who I am. Well, my name is Sarah J. Pitts. I've been coaching fitness since I was 13 years old when I would assist my high school PE teachers with lunchtime and extracurricular sports for the kids who were younger than me.

You'll learn more about my expertise and experience as we go through this guide, however, I want you to know that I've also been assessing movement treating and preventing injuries for over a decade. I've been on a mission for the last five years to create a simple solution for those coaches who want to do more to help their clients avoid injury without overstepping their role as a coach or being drawn into becoming a therapist.

For now, here's some facts about me. I've been in the industry since 1991. I've worked as a fitness instructor, personal trainer, corrective exercise specialist, and a soft tissue therapist. I'm the founder of mostmotion® and creator of the SMARTT® methods – the injury prevention approach that's changing the face of sports and fitness coaching.

I've helped countless individuals out of pain who have given up hope of ever finding a long-term solution. I've taught coaches across the world who are in turn, helping people out of pain and preventing countless more from developing pain in the first place.

I provide real solutions to the seemingly inevitable injury problem. I'm a massive dog lover and the proud owner of Belle, a cheeky, playful and a little bit bossy, Parson's terrier (we think), who is my "rescue rat bag".

Okay. Now you know what's coming and who is guiding you through this journey, let's just stop and imagine for a second what it would be like if you had a community that was consistent and religiously reliable in their attendance. Clients who seemed capable of achieving everything your programming threw at them and more, and who always arrived at your sessions excited and raring to go.

How amazing would it feel if you could create endless variety in your session, so you never run out of ideas? And made you look like the rock star coach you were destined to be? What if you were able to assess for and identify potential injury problems simply by watching your clients train? Your clients would think you had superpowers and be lining up to join your sessions.

What if you didn't have to change anything about how you coach and you could use your existing skills to start making a real difference? How about if you had a catalogue of ready-made videos available for your clients to follow that allowed you to charge much more than other coaches?

What if you had a step-by-step instruction that showed you exactly how to have everything I listed above?

What if you were part of a community of people who are all trying to achieve the same thing? What if there were training programmes, certifications and tools that would help you hit the ground running? What if? What if this is your solution?

* * *

INJURY PREVENTION LESSONS FROM THE DOG WHISPERER?

All my life I wanted to have a dog. When I was little, my parents would give reasons not to have one, like they were too tying, they would chew the furniture or leave hairs everywhere.

I don't know what it is about them, but to be honest, I'd rather be around dogs than people most of the time! I find animal behaviour fascinating, so when I discovered the TV show "The Dog Whisperer" with Cesar Millan, I was captivated.

I know, I know, right now you might be thinking "come on, Sarah, enough with the dogs, just show me how to prevent injuries", but there's something fundamental about treating injuries, that I learned from watching how Cesar Millan works to rehabilitate dogs with behavioural problems and educate their owners, and it's _fundamental to your success with preventing injuries_.

I'm going to do everything I can to show you the way. You're going to have the entire blueprint. You're going to know the systems, the tools, the methods that you need to prevent injuries in your clients. I'll reveal everything to you. However, the principles taught in the next few pages are what you need to understand to be successful with your injury prevention efforts.

I've dedicated my life to mastering these strategies, perfecting these methods and crafting these programmes so that you can make a difference with injury prevention, you're going to reach levels of success you never dreamed possible. Once you implement these methods, strategies and blueprint, you will impact a sea of people if you do what I'm sharing with you.

In return, all I ask is just one small thing. My request is that you please share these principles with all the other sports or fitness coaches you are influencing. Even if it's just one friend, because while our individual efforts may change a few lives, when we all work together, we can create a real and lasting change across the world. Let's be SMARTT®. Let's do this together.

So, what are the injury prevention lessons from the Dog Whisperer? The fundamental principle that will give you the results you've never experienced before is this:

The Rehabilitation Principle: In his book "Cesar's Way", Millan describes the order in which he works to rehabilitate dogs.

"when a dog has issues, you can't begin to solve them by dealing with 'Columbus'. You have to start with the animal, then the dog, then the breed, and then work your way down to the name stencilled on the food dish"

When I read this, I was totally blown away. When it comes to injuries -and especially treating them, we humans always start with the name of the problem and try to work our way backwards from there.

I was working as a soft-tissue therapist at the time, treating everyone from triathletes competing on the international stage, to folks destined for knee replacement surgery and the pain of osteoarthritis, and as soon as I started looking at things differently, I started getting results on the treatment table that other therapists had struggled with, and according to my patients, in a fraction of the time!

I began to investigate the human being as an animal, and what traits we shared with others. I read about everything from physics and chemistry to energy medicine techniques, and I discovered that movement is a fundamental requirement of all living things, even down to a single celled bacterium.

So, taking movement as my starting point, I began to apply that to the human form. Instead of treating the specific symptom of the patient on the table, I worked to restore unrestricted movement to their joints.

My patients thought I was some kind of magician, because by focusing on this one task, not only did my patients' pain go away (often within a few minutes, and despite me never actually touching or going anywhere near the site of their pain), when I started to create movements for them to do at home, it actually stayed away.

And this is where it gets really exciting for you. It occurred to me that it didn't actually matter which symptoms my patients came to me complaining of, the process was always the same…restore unrestricted movement to the joints.

In every single case – bar none, the result was the same. The pain went away. But that made me question why we were waiting for the pain to happen in the first place. In fact, it was after I'd heard the same phrase for the umpteenth time from a patient that it occurred to me just how powerful the role of the coach really could be. The phrase my patients kept saying was "My pain came back a bit this week, but I did those movements you gave me, and it went away again".

Again, this made me question why, as an industry, we were waiting for pain to happen before doing anything about it. Standard industry practice for treating injuries was, and still is, focused on the symptom itself, but my experience was showing me that this was a very slow and minimally effective approach, leaving folks suffering for longer than was necessary and/or having the same problem return time and again. Not only that, but the standard process completely ignores the people who have the most power to prevent pain from happening in the first place...sports and fitness coaches!

"The Rehabilitation Principle" wasn't the only cue I took from The Dog Whisperer's methods. The following cues, combined with my experience gained from following "The Rehabilitation Principle" have created a hugely powerful series of steps that every single sports or fitness coach can use to help their clients or athletes avoid injury, no matter what their level of injury knowledge:

Instinct: All human beings have strong instincts when it comes to things like safety or not feeling very well. Yet when it comes to movement, the industry teaches us that our clients are moving badly, and that they need us to correct it, which is simply not true. This has led to generations of people who have lost all sense of connection with their own bodies. They can't tell the difference between problematic pain and fatigue, and by the time they reach the age of 40, they have no clue what pain-free unrestricted movement feels like. They just accept their increasingly sore, aching and stiff body as "getting old".

This means that they can't actually tell us about potential problems because either they aren't aware of it, or they don't consider it to be an issue (usually because their pain doesn't stop them from training).

Another powerful instinct across all animals is the avoidance of pain. Most treatment and even mobility approaches focus on the area of pain, some even using the idea that creating more pain will trigger the healing response in the tissue, which may create an improvement.

Again, it's my experience with every single patient, bar none, that a pain-free approach is not only faster, but much more effective, which has huge implications for you as a coach.

The Power of Intention: Injuries are not the responsibility of fitness coaches – and nor should they be. Working with our clients with the intention of fixing them, is leading us into very hot water.

Let me be clear here. When I say injuries, I mean anything that involves pain – even on a low-level. The treatment of pain is nothing to do with you as a coach, let's leave that to the medical professionals, but non-painful movement, now that's something you can get your teeth into!

If your intention is simply to improve non-painful movement, you're on solid ground with your role and therefore your legal requirements. If it happens to reduce or even get rid of your clients' pain – great! But getting rid of the pain should not be your intention.

Focus on success, not failure: The industry has taught us to pick up what our clients are doing wrong and help them to improve. But when we concentrate on our clients' failings, we're teaching them to think that they aren't good enough, or that they should trust our say so rather than their own bodies – and who wants a coach that makes them feel like *that*?

Claim what you want. If you're not getting the information you need from your clients, to help you make better decisions, don't blame them, find a different way. You'll see in the upcoming chapters how easily you can do this, even when your clients can't or won't tell you.

Don't work against Mother Nature. It's a fight you definitely won't win. Use what your clients are naturally doing to create easier, faster solutions.

Know when to apply certain energy: Any fool can copy movements and repeat explanations they may have heard. But to truly understand what you're doing, and why, when it comes to improving movement is the real skill that will change your clients' lives and your coaching practices.

The less I think the more I connect: Using logic to test an infinite number of movement restriction combinations takes too long. Remove the logic, let go of the idea of "correct" and allow your clients to feel, explore and experiment to get to the root cause quicker.

Don't be afraid to dream big. Fitness coaches have the power to play the lead role in the fight against injuries and change the face of the industry for good. If we work together.

Now you have the fundamentals in place, your job is to keep the injury gremlins at bay and have fun doing it!

✳ ✳ ✳

THE FIVE STEPS OF INJURY PREVENTION

This is everything a coach needs to prevent injuries and build up an indestructible business. These five steps will take your coaching to a level that others can't even imagine.

STEP #1 – BREAKING THE BARRIERS

1.1: CREATING DEEPER CONNECTIONS

Taking the strain: Resistance is not your clients' fault.

Before you can start with any injury prevention intervention, it's important that we know exactly what the conversation is that's going on inside your client's head, the conversation we're trying to have with them, and more importantly, the disconnect between the two.

In order to avoid injuries effectively, we need to get feedback from our clients about what's been happening since we saw them last. Even if we're restricted to asking our group at the start of each session to indicate if they have any injuries we should know about. But more often than not, we don't get the information we need to be able to help them best because they're either unwilling/unable to give it or they just don't see the relevance.

If we want to be successful in preventing injuries, it's no good simply accepting this and then when they do get injured, which they will, blaming them because they didn't tell us. But we can't exactly spend hours digging into their previous medical history either, so how can we get around this?

Firstly, we need to know who they are so we can make better decisions. How old are they? Are they male or female? What sport are they involved in? What level do they participate at? How frequently do they train? What do they do for a living? What responsibilities do they have outside of training? How much stress are they under right now?

Even if you're coaching groups, you can make a few generalisations and work from there. For example, do you coach and under-11 girls' hockey team, who are local league champions, and most of whom are heading off to high school in the coming months? Or do you coach a young at heart low impact fitness class a couple of times a week for retired men and women.

This might not seem important, but each group of people will have different reasons that influence what information you are, or are not, given as a coach.

1.1.1 Four Questions to Answer

Your clients need you to meet them where they are when it comes to feedback. They will always give you the best answer they can, so it's up to you to help them give you more if that's what you need.

To help you do that there are four questions to ask yourself at the start of any session, and an example of them being answered by the young at heart group we mentioned earlier.

Question One: What Are They Saying?

This group of retired men and women are telling me that they feel fine with exercise I'm giving them. Nobody mentioned any aches and pains when I asked them at the beginning, and nobody has identified that they are struggling.

Many coaches will accept this silence as being a good sign and continue with the session as planned. But when we explore the next question, you'll see the disconnect between them and you when you take this approach, and it's the identification of this disconnect that will help you to take more effective action.

Question Two: What Do They Really Mean?

Older people have a tendency to not want to be a burden. Sometimes even the fear of being a burden to someone else can lead them to staying quiet about their own problems or sacrificing what they really want or need. They're also less likely to disclose information to us about issues that trigger painful memories, and they are much more likely to put aches and pains down to old age, which means they don't consider them to be a relevant factor since they live with these issues all day, every day.

Understanding people, even a group of people for who they are and respecting their situation rather than prying into it is one of the fastest ways to develop deeper relationships with their clients, because they feel like you truly understand them, which increases their trust and rapport with you.

Question Three: What's Stopping Them or Getting In Their Way?

False beliefs about creating problems, worry about causing more damage than good, being perceived as weak or frail (which can have life changing implications), or previous surgery are all elements that can get in the way of this group of people making progress.

Once you've identified some of the limiting factors like these, you'll know exactly what steps to take to help your clients, giving them confidence and you the opportunity to alter your practices if, on reflection, they have the potential to make your clients feel worse.

Question Four: How Can I Help Them Break Through This?

Finding opportunities to turn their negatives into positives, create activities that are challenging, yet achievable, and create activities that remove their fears are all ways that you can help your clients to break through the barriers that are getting in their way.

Putting someone's fears to rest is a powerful thing to do, and in many cases that can be life changing. It makes them feel like they can take on the world, and that's all because of you. So, can you imagine how they would feel if you did all that without them having to voice their fears out loud. Taking the time to consider your actions gives you this power for every person in every session you coach.

1.2: CHANGING YOUR LANGUAGE

Changing your language is perhaps the simplest thing you can do to break through the barriers and develop deep, long-lasting connections with your clients...and it's free! I recently broadcast a Facebook Live video called *'How to Win At Injury Prevention In 60 Seconds Or Less.'* I've transcribed the video below for you, but if you'd like to watch it, you can find it at: https://bit.ly/preventin60

1.2.1 How to Win at Injury Prevention In 60 Seconds Or Less

Hey, I'm Sarah from mostmotion® and I'm here with another 'Mobility Matters: Simple Injury Prevention for Fitness Coaches'. This episode is for every fitness coach who is trying to help their clients get better results and avoid injury at the same time.

So how can we get better or injury prevention in such a short space of time? Well in a word **language**. Why? Because coaches rely on client feedback to help prevent injury and if they can't tell you what the problem is, then we have less ability to help. The biggest reason that clients can't give you this feedback is because they can't feel it in their bodies.

There is a disconnect between them and their bodies and partly, coaches are the problem. And the reason for that is because of the language that we use, and the actions that we take. What I mean by that is when we're taught to be fitness coaches, we're taught that we know the correct technique, we know how to keep people safe, and all that kind of stuff. And because we believe that when we go out into the world, and we're coaching our people, we use words like, "poor technique", "wrong", "dysfunctional movement", things like that.

And even if we don't use those particular words, we focus on "improving" technique. When we focus on improving something, we're implying that it's not good enough, so we are helping to propel this feeling in our clients that they don't know enough, or their movement isn't good enough.

And that means they start relying on us to tell them when they're moving "right". Which means they've lost that feeling. When they lose that feeling, it means they can't tell you about it. So, how can we fix this in a really, really short space of time?

Well, there's three particular ways. And I've just popped into my studio here so I can show you what I mean, as we're talking. So, I'm just going to have a stand up.

#1 – Emotional Connection or Mental Imagery

One of the easiest ways to get people to connect with their bodies, is to help them have an emotional connection to it or use mental imagery. For me, a split-stance position [one foot in front of the other, in standing] is a very, very common position that I use because it's very, very easy, but people often feel like they're gonna fall over.

They just don't feel stable in this position, especially when they're kneeling down. So, I will say things like, *"imagine somebody's going to push you over."* If they don't feel particularly stable in this position, it may well be that they need to hold on to a wall, or a chair or something like that, it may mean that they need to adjust their feet. But when we ask them to imagine something, are we asking them to have a feeling, like if they've got a slumped chest, for example, if we say something like, *"imagine you've done something and you're really proud of yourself"*.

When you feel really proud of yourself, the chest comes up, and it's language like that, that we can use very quickly to change our client's body position without having to bog them down with teaching points like "lift the chest", "squeeze this", "engage that", and all the 15 different teaching points that we tend to bombard our clients with, every time they do something.

#2 - ENCOURAGE Exploration of When They Feel The Problems

So, if I'm in this [split stance] position, and I want them to feel a stretch around here [front of the hip], or maybe down the inside of the thigh, then I would ask them to tell me what position they need to be in. So, it might be that they need to rotate through here [upper body], it might be that they need to lean away [to one side] like this. If I do that, I can feel that right down the inside of my thigh, and it feels the worst point of the stretch, it feels the most stretch. But if I go this way [opposite direction], it doesn't feel like a stretch at all. If we explore these different positions, like if I rotate here, and lean back this way, now I can feel it in the front of my hip here. And that feels like quite a big stretch, too. But it's this experience of being in these different places that allows our clients to feel that difference.

And when they can start feeling the difference in these big situations, they can start to identify the smaller differences. And that's when they can start to tell us about it earlier than when it becomes painful or becomes a problem. And that's the whole point of asking them to connect with their bodies more so that we can get that information out of them earlier on. It helps us to help them.

#3 – Remove The Word 'Should'

The third way that we can help our clients do this very, very quickly, is to remove the word 'should.' Okay, now, it's very, very common, and I've used it myself a lot. Lots and lots of coaches use it all the time. Clients will ask us, *"Where should I be feeling this?"* And if I'm in this [split stance] position, got my hips pushed forward, my front leg might be slightly bent. It's my intention that they feel it in the front of the hip. But sometimes the word 'should' comes out and we say *"you should be feeling it here."* And when our clients don't feel it in that place, that could be for whatever reason, they might be feeling it in their ankle, for example, when we say the word 'should', it makes them feel like they're wrong when they don't feel it where we said. So, what we can do is say things like, *"It's my intention that you feel it through here [front of the hip], position yourself so that you feel it there."* And it might be they need to rotate a bit and push [the hip] out this way [to one side], *"oh, now I can feel it there* [front of the hip]*"*.

These are very simple things that allow us to get much better feedback from our clients and that helps us win with injury prevention in a very short space of time. Because we're asking our clients to connect with their bodies. Again, they can detect those small changes, and they can feel the difference. And when they can feel it, they can say it or at least they've got a better chance of being able to say it anyway.

1.2.1 5 Tips For Changing Your Language

Here are some simple tips for you to implement with your clients.

1. **Be less prescriptive.** Let your clients find what works best for them.
2. **Use feelings and mental imagery**, so they start to connect emotionally with the movement. Tying a movement to a feeling makes it easy to recreate quickly.
3. **Encourage exploration and curiosity**. The positional movement might not be technically correct but will help them to experience what feels good or not, which means they can tell you about it more easily.
4. **Use what you see to guide variety**. Everyone follows instructions differently, so use the differences you see to encourage new ways of moving. Remember, you don't need to have all the answers as a coach.
5. **Keep things positive**. Your clients are usually trying their best, and if not, there's usually a deeper reason for that, that's nothing to do with you. Telling them that they're

doing it wrong or moving badly won't help. Instead, ask them to *"try it like this"*.

Seeing The Matrix, The Secret Ingredient

Seeing the matrix is like looking behind the curtain, you'll never see the world the same way again. You're going to see the hidden opportunities for you to help your clients without them ever mentioning problems that they're having. This shows you understand them. It shows you as an expert and builds the trust and rapport straight away.

You're going to see your guidelines as a coach in a whole new light so you can deepen your expertise in the field you already love and develop an entirely new weapon in your arsenal too!

You're going to know how to get results that other coaches struggle to even imagine. Simply by coaching your regular sessions, you're going to establish yourself as someone other professionals want to work with, you're going to be identified as someone your clients and their friends want to work with. And you be able to see how easily to keep your clients in consistent patterns of training without the disruption of injury.

Seeing the matrix builds confidence and excitement. Whether you're new to injury prevention or a seasoned pro, you've never seen anything like this before. **Seeing the matrix keeps you coaching.**

The industry wants to turn you into a mini therapist. But the real magic is what happens when we can clearly see how to blend these skills into every single movement your client makes - no injury knowledge required! This unique approach will do exactly that and make your coaching skills your true superpower.

1.3: INSIDER SECRETS

Here are some insider secrets to "breaking the barriers". Our exclusive, in-house strategies, which are driven by one core principle: Be excellent to each other.

1. **See beyond the words.** In many situations, words don't adequately describe how someone is feeling or what they're thinking. Learn to look for the real meaning behind what's being said.
2. **Make life as easy as possible for your clients** to do or give you what you need to help them.
3. **Keep your language simple.** People have got enough to think about these days without adding copious amounts of teaching points that your clients will only remember one or two of anyway. Keeping things simple will help

them focus on you and your session instead of worrying about work or family life.

4. **Keep your language positive**. Build your client's sense of achievement so they feel good about what they've done. They'll be berating themselves enough if they didn't do as well as they'd hoped. And if they are, it's easy for them to take even the smallest negative from you to heart. Keeping your language positive will change their belief from *"I can't"* to *"I can"* – or even better *"I did"*. That's what gets results.

5. The most important tactic: **don't blame your client for what the industry has created in them**. I have a whole section on this in the coming page where we'll cover the power of context, which is the most effective communication tool.

1.4: THE "EYES, EARS, ASK, GIVE" STRATEGY

This is how you build true connection. It's how to gain trust and rapport. I'm going to make the whole process of preventing injuries very easy for you. However, before I do, I want you to know that your biggest goal when you're working with clients is to filter out the noise. Become an observer first. This is how you discover what's really happening. A client can tell you one thing when their body is clearly saying another. If you can filter out the noise, you'll get to the real problem, which means that you can deal with what the client says, what they really mean, and the issues with the body all at the same time. Amazing, right? It's so important that you get this right.

Let me tell you when most coaches get this wrong.

Our fitness industry has been teaching our clients, through coaches words and actions, that they have bad technique, movement dysfunctions, where they should be feeling stretches and how hard to train for so long, that our clients have completely lost all connection with their own bodies.

Yet we rely on **their** words to inform **our** decisions. So, if you're doing any of these things, stop!

- Adapting your session based on what your clients say.
- Listening, not observing
- Asking lots of questions
- Talking at, not talking with
- Trying to lead your clients to the verbal feedback you need
- Focusing on the client's problems
- Waiting to start the session until you have all the information you need.

Here's the right way to do this.

Step One: Understand that what you hear isn't really what's wrong. Here's an example. *"I didn't have time this week"*. Time is a classic excuse that very rarely is the real problem.

Step Two: Don't accept the first thing you hear. Many coaches would jump in at this point to try and make the session shorter because they focused on what the client said. Instead, ask an open-ended question like *"what changed?"* This gives your client the chance to explain more or get things off their chest. But don't be drawn into this. Just let them talk. Humans have become way too reliant on words. But our clients need to be aware of their problems before they can explain them to us.

Step Three: Watch them move. Get your client doing something simple like walking, but not for the sake of it. observe them as they move. How are they holding themselves? Does their movement look comfortable? How do they feel? Do they feel stressed to you? Are they moving less comfortably than usual?

Their bodies will reveal clues about problems long before a client can ever explain them to us, we just need to learn to look a little bit closer. For example, if they walk around like they've got the weight of the world on their shoulders, or they're talking so much that you think they might burst, it's likely that they have a lot of stress in their lives right now. Your client might not recognise this. But using these clues can get beyond the words to show your client that you really understand them.

Step Four: Prioritise what you **see**. Take your observations first, then layer on what the client told you to determine your actions. For example, if you observe your client looking more slumped than usual, they look and feel like they've lost the usual spring in this step, and they've told you that things have been super busy at work, you might think that a slower pace gentle stretching session might be most appropriate for them. But still don't take action yet.

Step Five. Ask them what they want and give them it. It might sound obvious, but never assume you know what's best for your client. You might recognise what they need to release the tension but that can come in many forms. Let them tell you what they want, then give it to them with a healthy dose of what they need. Just forging ahead with a gentle stretch session, when your client would much prefer to punch something would only show them that you don't understand them. They might feel a bit better after stretching, but they probably wouldn't enjoy the session. The simple act of asking them beforehand, allows you to give them what they want and that shows them exactly how awesome you really are. When we layer on what you know they need, that takes you to a whole new level.

That's it. It really is that easy. Once you become good at this, you can adapt any session to give your clients exactly what they want **and** what they need. In fact, there's a video that demonstrates how this amazing process works. Again, I've transcribed it below, but you can watch it here: http://bit.ly/bestinjuryadvice

You'll see how I'm able to prioritise body language over words, involve the client and then deliver exactly what they wanted and more. Listen to the feedback I got at the end of the session.

1.4.1 The Best Injury Prevention Advice Ever?

Hey, I'm Sarah from mostmotion® and I'm here with another video for every sport and fitness coach who is trying to help their clients avoid injury and get better results at the same time.

So, is this the best injury prevention advice you have ever heard? Well, the question is, in order to prevent things happening, we need to be able to see the signs before there's a problem. It's a bit like, if you had a problem with your steering on your car, you wouldn't wait until the steering didn't work before taking it to the garage, you would notice that there was a problem with the steering and take it to the garage before that problem happened. And it's the same thing with when it comes to preventing injuries. And this is really going to help you in business.

Because when you can see things happening before your clients even notice them – that helps them to really trust you, and to really feel like you understand them. There's a strategy that I use that I call **Eyes, Ears, Ask, Give.** And I'm going to explain to you what the strategy is. And then I'm going to give you an example of it in action.

Okay, so this is a five step process. The first step is to understand that what you hear is not really what the problem is, okay? Now clients need to be aware of a problem before they can tell you about it. So, they will give you examples of things like *"I didn't have time to do my training this week."* But what they really mean is, they didn't have enough brain space to deal with it, they couldn't cope with any more stress to deal with it, or they just didn't give it enough priority, the time isn't really the problem.

When we understand that what we hear isn't necessarily the problem, then it helps us with the second step, which is to *"Not accept the first thing we hear."* If I had taken action on somebody telling me, *"I didn't have time this week"*, then my response might have been to create a shorter session.

And if my client can't cope with more stress, they're feeling overwhelmed, or there's too much other stuff going on in their life to be able to give your exercise their priority it needs, it doesn't matter how short that timescale is, they're still not going to do it. So, if we don't accept the first thing that we hear, then it helps us to get deal with the problem, the real problem rather than the problem that we're hearing about.

The third step is to watch your client move. Why? Because bodies will give you signals that there's a problem way before your client will even be able to explain it to you. Your client will focus on all the things that are happening in their life, before they will accept that they are too stressed. They will focus on how busy they are at work or problems that they're having in their relationships, how time consuming and tiring their kids are, you know, all the little things that are happening in their life. But it will take them maybe 10-15 minutes to acknowledge the fact that they're feeling stressed and overwhelmed.

But their body will tell you that right from the very first second. Because they will come to you like [meh] and their body language, their eyes, you know, if you look in their eyes, and there's no, you know, there's no spark, they just, they just feel flat. I call it losing that bounce - when you've lost your bounce it's like, you're just not happy about something, perhaps you can't necessarily put your finger on it, but the body is showing you that right from the very first second that you see them. And when we watch them move, we can look for these little clues that give us the information that we really need to be able to deliver what the client needs.

The fourth step is to prioritise then what we see, which is why the strategy is eyes first, ears second. We prioritise what we see, we know the body is overwhelmed. We know that the body is struggling with something and then we can layer on what were the client was telling us *"I didn't have time"* they might well say *"I feel a bit stressed"*, but we **still** don't take action at this fourth step. We need to prioritise what we see because the body will give us those clues, even if the client can't tell us.

But if we don't put this fifth step into action, again, everything can go wrong. So, it may well be that I see the body is overwhelmed. And I think, *"Oh, well, let's do a stretch session, let's allow the body to calm down. Let's keep everything on a low level"*. But when I ask the client what they want, the client goes, *"actually, I just really need to hit something"*. If you offer them a stretch session, that is not going to wash. Okay, they might feel better after the stretch session, but it's not what they want.

So, when we ask the client what they want, then we need to give it to them. And I really good example of this as a client I had a few years ago now, I'm going to call him Darren.

Darren was a high-flying executive in a big business, and they were going through a merger, there was a lot of stress in his life, his relationship with his wife was very strained, his kids were very young, so they were really time consuming. He came to our session and he said, *"You know, I've been really busy this week, I haven't really had time to do the programming that you set."*

I was personal training with him once a week, he was doing some stuff by himself a couple of times a week. He just felt really bad. He said, *"I feel terrible that I haven't done the exercise."* and he was just like, his whole body was just so miserable. His body language was just showing me that he felt so miserable. So, I accepted what he said. He did feel bad about not doing the exercise, but his body just was telling me that he felt so overwhelmed.

My immediate plan was to do a gentle stretch session, because I knew that his body wouldn't cope with too much more, but I said to him, *"what is it that you feel like doing today?"*, and he went *"I don't know, I think I just need to hit something."* So, having a martial arts background, I got some pads out.

We did some warming up and he hit started hitting the pads, and he started feeling a bit better. But the secret is not just giving the client what they want. That's not going to get you the results that you need. As coaches, we also need to give the client what they need. And that's a big difference. The client wanted to hit stuff, and I could have just pushed his body and pushed his body and pushed his body to a really high intensity boxing session.

Afterwards, he might have felt mentally better, but his body would still have been physically exhausted and overwhelmed. But then we layer on what the client needs. I added all these movements so that he was moving in different ways, his body was opening out, it was lengthening out and reducing the amount of tension in his body at the same time, the feedback that you get from that is amazing. And the results are amazing.

He said at the end of the session, *"that was exactly what I needed. I feel so much better than I did. I can't believe how good I feel now."*

Okay, he was tired, but he was also very relaxed. And that's the key. I gave him what he wanted, but also gave him what his body needed. And that's the secret to the "Eyes, Ears, Ask, Give" strategy. You need to give the client what they want, because it helps them to get engaged in your session but when you can layer it on with what they need as well, you get amazing, amazing results.

1.5: TRANSFORMING YOUR COMMUNICATION

Here are our in-house strategies to better communication:

1. You need compassion and insight. Master my "Eyes, Ears, Ask, Give" strategy. It works so very well. Eventually, you'll be able to transition into seeing what the client needs way before they say anything at all.
2. Make sure you practice it every day. At first, it's a challenge but once you get good at this, you will love it, then it can become a cornerstone of your coaching that helps you to deliver outstanding results fast.
3. Make sure you know your coaching boundaries ahead of time, you should always know whether you're working inside of your remit or not. It's amazing how many

coaches are venturing into dangerous territory without even realising it. That's why I created "The Vault of Injury Prevention Secrets Training". You're going to learn more about practical movement solutions in the next section. It's there that you'll realise how all of this comes into play.

4. Don't assume that you know best. I'm telling you. This is the biggest mistake I see coaches make when they try to master injury prevention. Don't do this. You have the secret now. Use it. People love having what they want. Learn to make this a habit. It's the best way to form a connection so that you can build the trust and rapport with your clients. Even in a group. Give them it. serve your people.

5. Make sure that you're prepared for a variety of situations. And you'll be able to pivot quickly without even missing a beat, which will make you look like a rockstar.

1.6: DAILY CHECKLIST

This is how you build deeper connections.

1. Practice eyes is asked give every single day, even when you're not coaching, you'll get super attuned, don't give up.
2. Don't assume you know best. Human bodies are way more than the muscles and bones that they're made up of. Every single client has had unique experiences in

their lives that can lead or may have already led to many number of problems. treat them like the unique and complex beings that they are.
3. Stay true to coaching. Always know your coaching boundaries and how you can best use them to help your clients prevent injury.
4. Invite your clients to have input and give feedback on multiple occasions throughout your session. It truly gives them a personal touch and creates a stronger bond between you. Yes, even if it's a group.
5. Share feedback from one group or client with another anonymously, of course. It can give them ideas of what to say, if they're struggling, and shows that others are getting results.
6. Always encourage clients to tell you how they feel at the end of your session. It helps you improve and shows them that you care.

❋ ❋ ❋

STEP #2: ACTIVATING STEALTH MODE

Forget everything you know about mobility and injury prevention. We're about to go deep into how you can help to prevent injury **without** spending time on mobility.

Do this right and you won't even need to have mobility in your sessions. Please listen to me closely. So many coaches come to me with preconceived ideas of what mobility is. Many of them have spent hours studying the industry's best practices.

Mobility is what they've been told they have to do to stay within their role as a coach when it comes to injuries. I've seen use and even taught many of these practices over the years and they can get results. They often use fancy gadgets and the latest science. But there's one little problem, you have to stop coaching to do them. If I asked 10, 100 or even 1000 coaches if they related to this, I'd be willing to bet that about 95% of them would absolutely agree...well, you'll always get a few that don't agree!

This is the big reason why injuries are more prevalent than ever. Why? Because we've entered an era of simplicity and expectation. Your clients just don't have the brain space for complexity anymore. They want short, simple, clear instructions. And with the amount of information that's out there on the internet now, they have expectations of you that are higher than ever before.

Gone are the days of coaches telling clients what to do and leaving it up to the client to get on with it. Now, there's increasing pressure on you to take the strain when your clients fall short, to help your clients get the results they want.

If they have less time than a few years ago, it's up to you to find short-cuts, loopholes or insights so that they can still fit in everything they need to so that they can be successful.

If you follow the process that I'm showing you in this guide, you will make your clients as bulletproof as it's humanly possible to make them when it comes to avoiding injury, but you have to follow everything I'm telling you. When you do follow this process, you don't need a dedicated mobility section of your session. You might not even need to ask your clients to spend any of their own time on it. You can simply get on with delivering your sessions like you used to before mobility became trendy.

The coaching session structure has been a standard way for decades, yet we can make it into the most powerful injury prevention tool you've ever seen. You will over deliver for your clients and they will know that you have their best interests at heart. Are you getting this? I hope you're having huge lightbulb moment right now. I call this your fitness coaching superpower. It's the way that you are truly going to make a difference to your clients lives. But it requires consistency and commitment.

The ultimate solution to being successful on a long-term basis with injury prevention is to have consistency with, and commitment to, it with every session you coach. In the coming pages I'm going to show you how you can easily take the strain of mobility/flexibility/prehab/call it what you like, off your clients, saving them time and effort. They will see that you are committed to helping them succeed and is the best way to build deep and lasting connections with them.

A triathlon coach friend of mine once said something to me years ago and I've never forgotten it. He said triathlon coaching is about much more than just swim, bike, run. And the same can be said for any sport or fitness coaching. When we coach people, we're dealing with much more than just the exercise inside of the session. We're responsible for all the extra elements that keep them training too, like warming up, cooling down, stretching, and recovering from training.

Coaches have been including these extra elements into our sessions for decades. The original intention was that they would help prevent injury, yet injury rates have been rising steadily for all that time, so clearly something isn't working, so we've been adding more elements, like mobility in the hope that this would solve the problem...but it hasn't. A quick Google search will tell you that injury rates are still rising – at a faster rate and with younger age groups than ever before.

We need to stop trying to add more to our sessions, get back to focusing on the training itself, yet deliver **real** injury prevention results. We need to take advantage of the most overlooked parts of our session structure so that you can take the pressure off your clients.

If we focus every element of our sessions on injury prevention, including warming up, cooling down, stretching and recovering from training, we can finally start to make **real** progress (and I don't mean just raising and lowering body temperature).

2.1: THE CHALLENGE: PUT YOUR MONEY WHERE YOUR MOUTH IS!

I was challenged to create one warmup, one cooldown and one recovery day routine for a group of runners over 40. We compared their usual, industry standard approach to the SMARTT® injury prevention methods. This is what happened.

The warmup: The runners' usual, industry standard activity was to jog gently for five minutes. The aim was to raise the heart rate and body temperature, and although this outcome was usually achieved, many of the runners claimed that their joints still felt a bit stiff, especially because they "getting older" as they put it.

They didn't enjoy running at a slow pace, so right from the start they weren't focused on the warmup itself, because they just wanted to get out running. Besides, many of them thought warming up this way for a run was pointless, because they believed that they'd just warm up if they were running normally. They would usually spend a total of five minutes warming up (and therefore attempting to prevent injury), but they considered effectiveness to be about a three out of five.

With the SMARTT® methods, we took the same activity of gentle jogging, and took the same 5-minute period, but applied the exclusive 3M Flow™ strategy. This is what we did:

The runners started in standing, putting one foot forwards of the other, with both legs straight. They then gently and slowly moved their hips in any direction they could think of. We used a variety of circles, figures of eight, side-to-side and forwards-backwards movements. We spent a minute like this before switching feet, so that the foot that started in front was now behind. Once the hip joints started to feel warmer, we stopped the hip movements and keeping the same stance, bent the upper body down towards the floor and upwards towards the ceiling (pushing the breastbone as high as possible). Again, spending about a minute on each side. For the final minute the runners jogged slowly, turning their feet alternately towards each other and away from each other as they ran.

The aim was to open the hips, improve shock absorption, raise heart rate and increased body temperature. The outcome was that clients felt much warmer than usual, their joints felt looser, and they all felt ready to run. Their attention on the session was high, because it felt like they were doing something with real purpose. So even though we spent the same amount of time five minutes focusing on preventing injury, they rated the effectiveness as five out of five, rather than three.

The cooldown: This the arguably the most wasted opportunity in fitness!

The runners described their usual, industry standard cooldown as more gentle jogging and a bit of stretching (although many of them often skipped this bit) so the average duration of a cooldown can range anywhere between zero and ten minutes.

The aim is usually to lower the heart rate and body temperature and to restore muscle length to what it was before the session started. The runners reported cooling down even if they didn't do a dedicated cooldown and that stretching often feels like a struggle. They usually felt exhausted from the session and sore for a few days afterwards. Their attention on the cooldown section of the session was low because they think they will cool down just by walking to the shower and stretching is uncomfortable, which they weren't in a rush to replicate.

The total number of minutes preventing injury at this point in the session with this standard approach, can range anywhere from zero to ten minutes and the runners rated the effectiveness anywhere from one to three stars out of five.

But with the SMARTT® methods, the outcome was totally different. Again, using a 3M Flow™ sequence, we spent the same ten-minute period focusing not just on decreasing body temperature and restoring muscle length, but on **improving** hip movement in all directions, so that the runners would be starting the next session better than this one.

The outcome was that the runners managed the movements easily. They found moving in different directions fun but challenging, **purposeful** and engaging. They reported feeling tired but relaxed after the session and not as sore in the following few days. Their attention on the cooldown section of their session was really high, so the 10 minutes we spent here preventing injury gained a five-star effectiveness rating.

The recovery session. This is where most clients commonly go rogue or "off plan".

The runners reported that their usual rest/recovery day consisted of total rest or a light, active recovery session which they, like a lot of athletes or clients struggle with. They don't like the feeling of not training and many hate the lack of structure offered by many coaches here.

The duration of a standard rest/recovery activity can be anywhere between nothing and 30 minutes, the aim of which is usually just to give their body a rest from the strain of their regular activity. The outcome is that our clients often feel rested but quickly feel fatigued when resuming exercise, or they just feel frustrated. Their attention on the session is low.

Not training is difficult for so many of our athletes/clients. Many of them use their training time as a way of taking time for themselves, or of forgetting about their daily struggles for a while. Some might even use it as a way of letting off steam and we take that away from them, they often override our decisions, pushing too hard on light activity, or thinking that it's an opportunity to catch up on sessions they might have missed during the week.

The total number of minutes our runners spent on their recovery day preventing injury ranged anywhere from zero to thirty minutes, but they rated the effectiveness as one star.

With the SMARTT® methods the runners followed a 3M Flow™ sequence, focused on improving their hip movement, which lasted 30 minutes. The aim was to improve hip movement in all directions, increase blood flow and help flush out toxins.

The outcome was that the runners felt rested and ready to train again. Not only that, but they felt like they had structure and a purpose to replace their lack of running. As a result, their attention on the recovery session was very high. They reported less of an urge to work too hard or try to "catch up" with training sessions they might have missed during the week and made better use of their downtime.

They spent a guaranteed 30 minutes doing injury prevention on their rest day and they rated the effectiveness as five stars.

If we compare the industry standard approach to the SMARTT® methods, we can see that it's much easier to put guaranteed injury prevention time into our clients' training plans, without overloading them with extra things, that they don't actually want to do, in their own time. With a 5-minute warmup, a 10-minute cooldown, and a 30-minute recovery day routine, we can easily have our clients spend two hours on injury prevention each week, without even trying.

The runners in this challenge found other benefits to focusing more on preventing injuries too. They felt less sore, like they had more energy, they felt less stressed because they didn't have to try and squeeze as much in, they were excited to train each day and their running felt easier and smoother.

Overall, the runners rated their experience with standard industry practices as being three stars, and their experience of the SMARTT® methods as five.

When you make your existing training time dual purpose like this, you're massively increasing your value as a coach...and we're creating a **real** injury prevention solution.

2.2: CHANGING LIVES THROUGH INJURY PREVENTION

Here's just a few examples of what they're achieving.

Chris is a personal trainer specialising in working with the elderly, those with complex health issues and learning difficulties. And simply by blending these injury prevention methods into regular exercise sessions, he's been able to help his clients build vital confidence in themselves and motivation to continue with their fitness despite the health challenges.

Like a client of his, Margaret, a 69-year-old client, who loved attending her Zumba class until they began to trigger her arthritis and motivation to exercise began to slip away because of her pain, which didn't help her type two diabetes. Chris created an appropriate 3M Flow™ warmup routine, which helped mobilise her joints so they were less painful. And this has been the trigger to give her the enthusiasm she needed to get back into regular exercising and keep her diabetes under control.

Then there's Jacqui. Jacqui is a World and European Champion age-group triathlete who works full-time, coaches part-time and tries to fit in her own training too. She was struggling to find time to fit in her own mobility training. but since she's been teaching and demonstrating the SMARTT® methods style of warming up and cooling down, using the 3M Flow™, she's found that she doesn't actually need to spend time on her own mobility at all. So not only is she helping prevent injuries with our own clients, but she's helping prevent her own too!

Shirley is a Pilates teacher who enjoys keeping herself fit doing triathlons. She teaches upwards of 20 Pilates sessions a week, but she says she felt almost ashamed that she was teaching a style of fitness that was supposed to prevent injury, yet she was injured herself. Since she's been blending the SMARTT® injury prevention methods into what she teaches, she's not struggling with our own injuries anymore. And many of her clients who are in their 60s and 70s are commenting on how much looser their bodies feel.

Martin is an outdoor adventure instructor who dislocated his shoulder white water rafting a few years ago. Since then, he struggled to demonstrate certain moves in a kayak and felt apprehensive of using his arm in certain positions, which is severely limited his ability to demonstrate activities. He's been using the SMARTT® injury prevention methods to improve his own range of movement in his shoulder and those of his clients so that he can demonstrate confidently again and prevent his clients from suffering the same fate that he did.

2.3: WHAT'S THE SECRET?

The secret to successful, long term injury prevention, is ultimately getting more results for your tribe with every single session.

I'm going to introduce you to a concept that will forever change everything about your coaching is a concept that I've mastered, not just with my students, but also in life. Are you ready for that concept?

Stealth Mode

"Taking place in secret", that's the official definition from yourdictionary.com. I like to refer to it as gift wrapping. In other words, we're going to make it very easy and fun for your clients to take action with preventing injury.

The action could be simply as simple as adding movement to the stretches they already know and use at home.

By the way, that is the most that is one of the most effective ways to help your clients get started helping themselves when it comes to preventing injury.

Your clients succeed when they're consistent, like brushing their teeth, or eating the right vegetables or training and they're much more likely to do the things **they like** doing (like training), then they are likely to do things they **don't** like doing (like stretching). But the magic happens when you disguise the things they don't like doing, as the things they do!

It's a bit like when you try to get kids to eat vegetables. If you really had to hide the vegetables, you could whizz them up in a blender to make a delicious, really thick and tasty pasta sauce. The children (and many adults) would eat and enjoy the pasta, completely oblivious to the fact it was packed full of things they supposedly didn't like.

Or you could make a pizza base out of cauliflower. That way, they still feel like they're having pizza, but they're also getting the vegetables. Or you can make their favourite brownies with sweet potato, or chocolate cake with beetroot...the list goes on, and I'm sure you're getting the idea.

2.4: HOW TO MAKE INJURY PREVENTION EASY

Pretty incredible, right? There was no such system on the planet, so I had to create it myself. I'm not saying that to brag, I just couldn't find anything that came close to what I was looking for.

I wanted a system that allowed coaches to give clients what they wanted, which is to get on with training, at the same time as delivering what they needed, which is injury prevention.

I wanted to be able to get results in a few minutes, not hours, and I wanted to be able to use these methods anywhere without equipment. I wanted anybody of any age, movement capability, or understanding to be able to use these methods.

I wanted to be able to use movements that were easy to do not have clients worry that they will be doing them wrong. I wanted big groups to be able to use the same movements yet still customise them to suit their own needs.

I wanted coaches to be able to become a big part of the injury conversation - regardless of their level of experience or knowledge of injuries.

I wanted clients to stop having to pay out endless amounts for ongoing treatment, injury management or "maintenance" treatment sessions.

I wanted upcoming stars to be able to fulfil their potential, not drop out due to injury and I wanted to end the inevitability of sporting injuries across the world.

I simply couldn't find it, so I had to create my own solution and you're going to hear about it later on in the chapters.

I created a brand-new solution that makes injury prevention easy. Now you can say goodbye to foam rolling, stretching and resistance bands. We'll talk more about this system in later chapters. Just know that it's everything that you've been looking for.

✳ ✳ ✳

STEP #3: BUILDING YOUR SUPERPOWERS

This is how your clients become injury resistant...it's time to get specific.

Now your clients are being consistent with their injury prevention, it's time to take your coaching and their results to a level that other coaches really struggle to imagine. We're going to take all your clients' technique and performance problems away without spending hours on drills or endless repetition.

If we want our clients to become resilient, we have to stop being generic.

When you follow this process, you will already have started helping your clients to feel better in their movements and very little technique specific time will be necessary.

Breaking skills down into individual drills is optional, but not really needed to build strength, protect joints, improve technique, improve movement, efficiency, and reduce wear and tear on joints. If you do this right, your clients won't need to spend time on their technique problems. Drills and repetition are for those people who don't understand how nature works or haven't appreciated their clients for the individuals that they are.

3.1: YOU GET THE BEST RESULTS FROM STRENGTH TRAINING – IF YOU DO IT RIGHT

Most coaches think that adding weights to movements like squats will protect their clients joints from injury, and it will to a certain extent. The problem is that traditional strength training uses movements that must be done the "correct" way, which means high volumes of repetition, and progression is measured through the amount of weight a person can lift safely.

This excessive repetition at the expense of other ways of moving joints and under increasing weight means that we aren't building resilience into our clients' joints, we're simply building stiffness around the joints so they can't move in any other way. And to make things worse, in most cases, not enough consideration is given to the client's **existing** individual movement habits, which means that this stiffness is built on top of these existing issues, as a coach is focused on getting the exercise movement "right".

At first, the stiffness seems to support the joints. But soon these underlying individual movement habits start to show through the cracks, and they start to create problems, especially when the joints are being asked to move in different ways all of a sudden, like a runner, tripping over a tree root when running through the woods, or a weight slipping at the bottom of a back squat, for example.

I've lost count of the number of clients I've dealt with have developed pain after strength training in this way, so pay attention to what I'm about to tell you when it comes to strength training!

I've spent over 30 years in the fitness industry, participating, coaching, rehabilitating and treating injury. I've seen strength training techniques develop and trends come and go so I know a thing or two about the impact that current strength training techniques have on the human body.

3.2: STRENGTH + VARIETY = RESILIENCE

Variety of movement is your most powerful injury prevention weapon...If they can bend, they won't break!

Here's my 5-point plan for building injury resilience into your clients' training:

- Add as much variety as possible to every single strength training exercise. It's very common for me to add at least six variations in every single session. I've identified over 200 possible variations for any given exercise.
- Make sure you identify the underlying movement issue that your client is struggling with and base all your programming around it.
- Industry standard correct techniques are good when you're trying to compete or perform assessments. But they're not great for preventing injury. There's no way to cater for individual needs when you're always looking for the correct. You will, however, make small improvements to technique and performance.
- When you focus your strength training around your client's individual needs and combine it with variety of movement, you will blow up your clients' results and you will help protect them from injury.
- I have a strategy called the "Silent Performance Gremlin Eliminator" which is going to double or triple your clients' performance results once you start using it.

Traditional strength training methods are losing popularity. I'm now going to introduce you to my super results generation formula.

3.3: THE RESULTS GENERATION FORMULA

What if you could improve your clients' technique and performance faster and with less effort? Like these guys and gals.

Fiona Hoare, triathlon coach, says *"This has encouraged me to broaden my horizons and think outside the box. Rather than using the standard one glove fits all approach is very refreshing"*.

Martin Higgins, outdoor adventure coach, says *"this has given me the tools and confidence to improve my clients' performance in ways that are only ever hinted at by mainstream coaching and physiotherapy. The results are fast, effective and life changing, not just in athletic performance."*

Margaret Sills, triathlon coach, says *"this approach should be the cornerstone of fitness coaching education. I love how my thinking can get straight to the heart of the problem without overwhelming or confusing my clients."*

The Super Results Generation Formula is the fastest route to results you've ever seen. Follow this outline to get super loyal, consistent and injury resilient clients, even if they're brand new to you.

1. From the start, make it clear that your clients are going to achieve a specific result, like make swimming or running or squatting feel easier or faster or more powerful.
2. Set out a 30-day timeframe to deliver this result. You might not need that long. But this timeframe gives you time to show just how effective your coaching is.
3. You include a weekly coaching call to help you engage with the client and keep programming on track to deliver maximum results.
4. One of the most effective ways to get results is to do it with them. Follow-along videos are a great way to do this saving you time while your client feels more connected to you.
5. Identify which one of the 3 Silent Performance Gremlins (SPG), that underpins every non-specific or gradual onset injury, is impacting your client the most
6. Focus every warmup, cooldown, recovery day, skill acquisition and strength training session within the 30-day period around improving the identified SPG, then ask them if they're satisfied with the outcome. If so, ask them if they'd like to continue training with you.

Make sure you deploy this "Silent Performance Gremlin Eliminator" strategy during the first 30 days of working with every new client. It will double or triple their results, and often give some surprising additional benefits too.

3.4: CASE STUDY: CHRIS YATES

When I first started working with "Yasmin" she was struggling with persistently tight hamstrings and a numbness in a little toe that was preventing her from walking very far, driving and doing other tasks of normal daily life.

She wasn't sleeping very well couldn't run and struggled to relax but was using exercise to manage your stress levels. During my initial assessment, it would have been easy to miss her subtle movement restrictions. She had a good posture, good alignment and standing and a comfortable gait. She also had reasonable balance.

But using the "Silent Performance Gremlins Eliminator" strategy, I was able to identify two main areas that were likely to be contributing to her symptoms and restricting her daily life.

Yasmin was happy attending group classes for her main exercise sessions, so I created a series of warm up, cooldown and recovery routines for her to follow that helped her to deal specifically with her individual issues.

At first, Yasmin was simply doing the classes because she felt that they were helping, but when we started dialling into her specific issues, she noticed that she'd been overexerting herself and was able to make the informed decision to switch her approach to something more suitable to her.

Since her problems have been ongoing for a while, she's also seeing a physio and undergoing tests from the doctor. At first, I was a bit nervous working within a team like this, but I quickly realised that we were all working on differing, yet complimentary approaches, which gave me the confidence to continue.

Within the course of her 30-day programme, Yasmin is now making more appropriate decisions regarding the intensity of her fitness. She's sleeping much better, she can drive her car, walk and live her daily life without discomfort, and she feels like the numbness in her foot is improving. Running beyond one kilometre is a work in progress, and she's still waiting for a doctor's appointment.

* * *

STEP #4: CONNECTING THE DOTS – STEPPING INTO YOUR FULL POTENTIAL

Many of our clients struggle with constant, low-level pain or underlying conditions that they themselves might not even be aware of. If you can help these clients to move without pain, you'll quickly establish yourself as a real expert in your field, you'll build a loyal and eager client base, and providing unrivalled results – which ultimately will lead to more revenue.

This isn't going to happen overnight though. You need to have consistency and commitment to build a really strong coaching identity based on injury prevention, and to grow your tribe of eager and capable clients. But I can guarantee that if you do everything I outlined in this guide, you're going to be in that position. Show your clients that you can get results, and then do it again. And again. And again.

Here's what's so amazing. If you're willing to go all in...
You have that consistency and commitment each and every day.

You're putting your clients' movement needs first

You demonstrate that your head and shoulders above every other coach out there.

You're providing so much more than just training requirements.

You're Mastering the Art of injury prevention.

You get your clients results faster and easier than ever.

You are positioning yourself as a trusted and respected professional in the eyes of other professionals

I can guarantee they will be the most loyal and consistent clients you've ever had. And you won't have the hassle of finding new clients, they'll start finding you.

4.1: TAKING YOUR COACHING TO THE NEXT LEVEL

There are three factors of pain or injury, yet most professionals only focus on one or two.

When I refer to connecting the dots, I'm talking about understanding the factors that combine to create injury and your place in the middle of it. Most coaches won't ever reach this level of understanding, but they're missing a huge opportunity.

I've identified three main factors that converge when it comes to pain/injuries, and fitness training.

1. **The body** - This is what the majority of the industry focuses on. But it's not the complete picture. What's happening with muscles, bones, connective tissue and the tightness within the body is only part of the story.
2. **The mind** - How a client feels about their pain, and/or previous pain is a powerful influence on the third factor.
3. **Action** - What is happening in the client's body and mind will dictate what actions they will and won't take when it comes to their training.

Understanding each of these factors and how they converge into the motivation, confidence and performance of your clients will take your coaching to a level that most other coaches won't even consider – and that **puts you at a massive advantage**.

When we consider which professionals focus on which of the three factors individually, it's easy to see where the gaps are and as a result, it's clear to see how fragmented the industry really is.

Body. Physical Therapists, body workers and specialist Fitness Trainers focus here

Mind: Behavioural therapists, psychotherapists and counsellors focus here.

Action: All sports and fitness coaches focus on this regardless of their level of understanding of injury.

Specialist Fitness Trainers and physical therapists try to connect the body with action, but often exclude the mind component which results in limited or temporary results.

When we start connecting the dots, we take care to understand what other professionals are trained to achieve, the toll of pain (or even the experience of previous pain) on our clients and what we can do to ease the situation for everyone involved.

Connecting the Dots means understanding the world around you. This is how you stand head and shoulders above the crowd of other sports and fitness coaches.

Most fitness industry standard courses that deal with injuries drag coaches away from coaching and into hands on treatment. The SMARTT® Methods are not that.

You've already seen in this guide just how much faster and easier you can improve your client's movement, technique and performance by following these steps. Now it's time to show everyone just how capable you are...without becoming something you're not.

This means understanding where other professionals are coming from so you can see how you can help them, and you can demonstrate how:

- Medical professionals don't need to spend time explaining details to you, which shows you understand them.
- You're not trying to duplicate their work or disrupt it which helps you build trust.
- You are complimentary to them, which increases referrals to you
- You can help clients easily understand what's happening in their bodies shows knowledge and expertise without the jargon

- Increases compliance from clients which makes you look good in the eyes of other professionals.

One of the biggest barriers to successful injury prevention is the technical jargon. It's confusing and sometimes daunting for clients and puts many coaches off even trying to get involved. But one of the most important things you need to understand about the medical language is that it's only necessary for the medical professionals, **not you**.

As coaches, it's helpful for us to understand what it means, but it's not what will ultimately drive our actions. We use a system that helps us to keep our focus simple, on our actions effective. It's what I call the "Whole Human Method". We will get into this method, but first, let me tell you a quick story about how we ended up here.

4.2: WHEN CONNECTING THE DOTS FAILS

In 2001, I was physically assaulted in my own home. My back was so bruised, that I could hardly stand upright, and a black horizontal line highlighting my on my skin where each of my vertebrae was. As a young 20 something year old, recently graduated from university. I'd been out drinking some friends earlier in the evening and gone home to bed. I don't remember exactly what happened. But I do remember being in my PJs in my housemate's bedroom being hit by her partner.

It was no secret that I didn't like the woman she was seeing. She was a bully and controlling and I've made it clear to my housemate that I didn't want her in the house. Yet here she was standing over me in my own house, repeatedly punching me while all I could do was curl over in an attempt to protect myself.

I still don't know to this day why I was in my housemate's bedroom, or why her partner was there. But I had this feeling in my gut that somehow, I had brought this fight on myself.

I was so filled with shame that I didn't tell a soul. The only people that knew my housemate and a friend who offered to take me to her martial arts classes.

Over the next couple of weeks, my body healed, and I began to regain some of my confidence through the martial arts training. A few months later, I moved away from that town and never looked back.

I didn't think about the assault much over the next few years. But within a year or two, I tore my hamstring and began struggling with back pain.

Of course, I didn't know then what I know now about injuries, so I was relying on other people to help me deal with them. It was then that someone offered to do a spinal adjustment. Unfortunately, this, combined with a different treatment I was having my hamstring, strained the ligaments in my spine and I was in agony for a few weeks.

After this settled, I began developing little nagging problems in my knee, hip, and shoulder. But despite trying many conventional treatments, my body seemed far too sensitive to cope with any of them. Afterwards, I always ended up feeling worse than before.

I've always been fit and active my whole life. But around 2012 I started noticing after intense exercise, my body would just shake, like I'd had too much caffeine, and it would take ages to settle.

Gradually as my work stress increased. This reaction to intense exercise got worse, so I ended up not really training at all.

It felt like nobody understood what was happening and I felt like I was going to training but not really putting any effort in, which made me miserable.

It's not surprising, given that all this was happening to me, that the focus of my entire career has been injuries and during the same timeframe, I progressed from being a fitness instructor, to a personal trainer, to rehabilitation assistant in the NHS, to a corrective exercise specialist, to a soft tissue therapist in an attempt to help people like me, who seem to be suffering from persistent and nagging injury issues.

But it wasn't until I spoke to what seemed like the umpteenth therapist about my injuries, that it was suggested that my body's extreme reaction to treatment wasn't normal, and it was similar to those suffering from PTSD.

This new information changed everything for me.

It helped me understand why my body wasn't tolerating high intensity exercise, why I'd struggled with all those nagging injuries, and why I was being so sensitive to treatment. But not just that, it also helped me understand smaller behavioural changes I'd begun to notice. Like being completely demotivated by fitness coaches shouting (to the point where I wanted to leave the session) or digging my heels in and refusing to add more weight to my bar in a group class (and almost having a standard argument about it in front of everyone).

I'd even become super sensitive to changes in atmosphere, to the point where I knew a fight was brewing in a pub before it happened and insisting to my friends that we must leave immediately.

I'll admit, I've kept this information about myself under lock and key for many years and even now – sharing this with you isn't the easiest thing for me to do (I only plucked up the courage to tell my parents a few months ago), but I hope it highlights just the kind of deeply personal and hugely relevant information that our clients **don't** share with us as coaches.

We focus on the sport or movement patterns of our clients' bodies and sometimes we're unknowingly expecting our clients lack of motivation, or in consistencies to be something to do with our programming, or some kind of physical issue.

If I was your client right now, and you didn't know this about me (which is likely because I wouldn't have wanted to tell anyone, even you), it's most likely we'd be parting ways before long – you'd likely get frustrated at my apparent lack of effort, or inconsistent training patterns, and I'd get demotivated by my own lack of progress. At best, I might tag along at the back of a group exercise class, where I'm less likely to be noticed, slowly getting demoralised at my own inconsistent capabilities…and even if you did have this information about me as your client, what could you even do about it?

If my experience of my own injuries and over 15 years of coaching and treating other people with injuries has taught me anything – it's that the whole system is very fragmented – and that's why it's not working.

Each professional involved is responsible for their own specialty and each of them is trying their best to improve the client's situation given what they know. The problem is that the one person who knows least about the situation is the one that's being relied on for all the information...the client!

Our clients try their best to remember what they've been told by other professionals. They try to remember the technical jargon in the hope that it will make our lives as coaches easier, but when it comes down to it, if they don't understand what they've been told, mistakes are easily made.

I've lost count of the times a client said to me something like 'medial hamstring' and when I've asked them to point at where their pain is, they're pointing at their elbow or somewhere.

And if we add to that the fact that the fitness industry has us constantly reminding our clients that they move badly (by focusing on improving technique, or using phrases like "dysfunctional"), or asking them to ignore what they're feeling - pushing them to do "just one more" when they want to stop, it's hardly surprising that they don't trust themselves to make a decision about their own bodies.

That also leaves them in the horrible situation of having to coordinate to three or even more professionals, which is time consuming, tiring, and sometimes confusing if those professionals have slightly conflicting ideas, or worse, no idea of what to do to help. As a client once reminded me:

"I don't want to have to think, I just want one person to tell me what to do!"

That's why I created my **Whole Human Method.** I'm going to reveal that to you here shortly, but it reminds coaches of all levels to acknowledge that there are more powerful forces at play than we can ever comprehend, with each and every single one of our clients. And as sports and fitness coaches, we are in the very <u>best</u> position to be able to do something to improve things for everyone involved.

Body orientated (or physical) therapists aren't that different to us. They can also specialise in their area of interest. For some of them it's late-stage physical rehabilitation which branches out into exercise, but there's so many of them who hate doing this with patients and would jump at the chance to leave their patients in the capable hands of an exercise professional who understands the treatment plan, so they don't have to spend ages explaining the ins and outs of each patient's case.

And of course, mind orientated therapists working on an emotional level with patients have this ability to specialise too. Many will use exercise as a way to alleviate symptoms of anxiety and depression, but there are many more who prefer not to learn about this because it's not their area of interest. Those therapists would prefer to let an exercise professional handle this, but again, one who understands the treatment plan.

Until now, sports and fitness coaches haven't had the opportunity to bridge this gap. They have been pushed into choosing one main area of specialism. For some, that has been the physical aspect of exercise and for others it has been mental health, but there are many more of us who recognise that there's so much more to coaching sports and fitness than just one thing.

That's where the Whole Human Method really comes into its own. By understanding **both** the physical and emotional sides to injury, you can be that one person, that bridge supporting your clients in all aspects of their injury issues - without once treading on other professionals' toes or stopping the coaching that you love so much.

4.3: THE WHOLE HUMAN METHOD – 3 CONVERGING FACTORS

Here's how this works. The goal of the Whole Human Method is to become the bridge between the therapy world (both physical and emotional), and your client.

Just because you become a bridge does not mean that you have to go and qualify in each discipline. Instead, we understand what the goals of each discipline are, the language that they speak, and translate it into what we do as coaches. That way, we're complementing what each of these therapies is trying to achieve, not duplicating or disrupting them.

Bridging bodywork means understanding what the physical therapist is trying to achieve with their hands-on soft tissue treatment and translating it into non painful movement. This helps your client to build a positive experience about moving their bodies in ways that have previously caused them pain, which means helping to *remove the emotional barriers* that may be preventing their bodies from moving easily and which may be contributing to their levels of pain.

Bridging mind work means understanding that your clients may have lived through previous trauma or having high levels of anxiety that are limiting their abilities to achieve their fitness goals. translating this understanding into non painful movements that allow them to explore and gently *push the boundaries of their own movement* can help to reframe the mind's reaction to being in certain positions or moving in certain ways that have previously caused pain or anxiety.

Complementing other professionals in this way adds massive value to your services and it's at this point that all kinds of magical things start to happen. Not only do your clients get the straightforward, simple instruction they were desperate for, but other professionals will start to notice the unusually big jumps in improvement that those clients are making between sessions.

When something out of the ordinary starts happening, questions start being asked, and YOU start to get noticed. Your results start to speak for themselves and even though they may never have met you, or even spoken to you, referrals will start coming your way.

Your clients will no longer have the burden of having to relay complex technical information about their condition. I've even had clients say things like, "I don't know how she does it. All I'm doing is moving a bit like this and it's helping".

4.4: A UNIQUE SOLUTION

Are you starting to understand what's been created here? Everything has been created from a need in my own business and frustrations with the system as a whole. My clients wanted **one** person to tell them what to do. That way they didn't have the burden of having to relay technical messages or worrying that they might not get some of it right.

I wanted to be able to pass my treatment clients on to a fitness coach who understood what I was trying to do and could help our mutual clients do more of it, without replicating my treatment or disrupting it.

I wanted my clients' coaches to understand the impact that the lingering effects of trauma was having on their bodies, and the programming implications that had. Particularly on the level of intensity of exercise that clients could cope with.

I wanted my clients to do more to help themselves outside of the treatment room and the best time to do that was when they were already doing something active.

I wanted fitness coaches to stop being ignored when it comes to the injury conversation and help them become the valuable piece of the puzzle that they are.

I wanted any sports or fitness coach to be able to make a safe and effective contribution to the injury process, regardless of their level of certification.

Finally, I wanted a way for all sports and fitness coaches to be able to communicate easily with medical professionals, to break down the barriers and get millions more caring individuals involved in helping clients avoid injuries...I mean, let's face it, nobody actually wants anyone to suffer with injuries, do they?

I had a vision, and I created a way for it to happen:

Make sporting injuries the exception rather than the rule.

We'll talk about more about this solution in the later chapters. Just know that it's absolutely phenomenal.

* * *

STEP #5: BECOMING INDISPENSABLE

This is where it all comes together.

Look at everything you've learned - amazing strategies, right? You've also learned about the different levels that mastering injury prevention can take you to. I'm almost ready to give you a sneak peek into the suite of training I've created to show you how to achieve all of this but first I wanted to make sure you understand something.

All of these things we've covered:
- truly understanding your clients
- safeguarding yourself as a coach
- exploiting overlooked areas of your session to maximise your clients results
- easily eliminating technique and performance problems
- lightning-fast assessments
- becoming the communication bridge between other professionals and your clients.

These are all things that we've been talking about in this guide. But to see this vision achieved in all its glory, we need clients and therapists to become part of the equation.

What if you and I could work side by side to help you create your own referral network. This would mean that you'd be connecting with the most appropriate complimentary professionals and bringing more clients to you.

You could then work in a wonderful harmony to make huge differences to your clients lives. And the best bit is that they would be exactly the kind of clients that you love working with!

5.1: THE COMMUNICATION NETWORK

Only those dedicated of coaches will want to join forces with other professionals to create a seamless collaboration environment and that means that it won't be for everyone, but that doesn't mean that other coaches have to miss out.

True collaboration means identifying the skills and abilities of everyone involved and creating a unique environment where they can all contribute.

To show you what this might look like in practice, let's use the example of an imaginary sports club called Resultsville Triathlon Club. There are about twenty coaches at Resultsville, all at different levels of triathlon coaching certification. Here are just a few:

Judy is a parent volunteer, who got into coaching as a way of helping out while her son was training. At the moment, she's an assistant coach which means she can only help out when she's being supervised.

Mike is qualified to run sessions by himself and got into coaching because he got bitten by the triathlon bug and wanted to help others have the same experience he did.

Sally is a Personal Trainer as her main job and helps to run the strength and conditioning sessions at the club and **Tim** is the club injury nerd. Like Sally, he's also a professional coach as his main job, training triathletes for their first Ironman but loves everything to do with rehabilitating injuries.

Without a simple way to communicate about injuries, the triathletes at Resultsville must be referred to **Jane** (the Physio where club members get a discount), or to Tim, the injury specialist. The other coaches have no clue how to help and must not get involved.

To try to help the situation, Tim delivers an in-house training to all the Resultsville coaches, showing them some of what he knows about injuries...but this type of third-hand information is dangerous for everyone involved.

Everything Tim teaches at this in-house training puts Judy, Mike and Sally **outside** of their coaching guidelines, which puts them at risk if anything were to go wrong as a result. And since Tim was the one delivering the training, he would also be held responsible.

The industry is very clear on this...and for good reason. Injuries are a complex subject that are NOT the responsibility of non-specialist coaches. It's a bit like thinking you can do brain surgery because you know how to hold a scalpel!

But this means that the pressure of dealing with all the injuries in the club is down to just TWO people, Tim and Jane. All the other coaches want to help, and the club wants to reduce the injury rates of their members so how can they do that without overstepping their coaching boundaries?

Simple. Give everyone a job they CAN do...even a brain surgeon needs someone to pass the scalpel!

Judy, the coach with the least experience and qualifications can use her observation skills to spot potential injuries to her supervisors and more qualified coaches, which makes her feel really useful while she gets to grips with learning to coach.

Mike, the qualified group triathlon coach can use movement in the warmups, cooldowns and recovery sessions to improve joint movement and reduce the restrictions that lead to injury, which makes him feel part of a team.

Sally, the strength & conditioning coach can create strength sessions that continue Mike's work to keep the joints open, building resilience into the Resultsville triathletes, and Tim can be the bridge between Jane (the Physio) and the other coaches in the club.

Now, ALL the coaches in the club can contribute to the prevention of injuries, each with a very clear and specific role that's well within their coaching guidelines and helps to divide the workload across twenty people rather than leaving it to just two.

At this point, some coaches might be concerned that Jane will lose business, but far from it. The word quickly gets out that she gets results with treating injuries faster than other Physios (because she's working alongside Tim), so she's busier than ever – but she still gets to focus on the hands-on treatment that she loves. Tim is busy too because he's doing the rehabilitation work for Jane, and the club is attracting new members because the public perceive them as being more caring and a safer place to train.

Of course, I used the example of a sports club to demonstrate how this works in practice because many of us are familiar with how a club is structured, but when you have a simple way to communicate, your ecosystem can be in any location, in any sports club or fitness business, anywhere in the world (providing you have a good internet connection).

Wherever you are on your coaching journey, being part of an ecosystem like this is how you will become an indispensable part of preventing injuries, but building your own ecosystem, helps you to establish and future proof your business.

Teamwork makes the dream work.

* * *

INTRODUCING THE SMARTT® METHODS

The SMARTT® methods are the only approach sports and fitness coaches need to help prevent injury.

In 2012, I began to realise that there wasn't really a way for me as individual therapist to take care of my clients through the entire injury process from pain to never coming back again.

Clients would come for treatment until the pain stopped and then they would go back to training or reduce their session frequency so that the amount of training they were doing was counteracting the progress we were making in their sessions.

I just wanted a way of helping my clients get rid of their recurring injury problems completely. Now, I can help my clients do what used to take months, in a few days. The only reason why is because of the system I built for my own business. It's the fastest and simplest path to results you've ever seen.

I also wanted a way to be able to simplify information, compliment other professionals and create a more cohesive approach to the whole injury problem. There wasn't anything available to do what I wanted to achieve, so I created it. I call that approach the **"SMARTT® Methods"**

There's communication and coaching analysis training, which allows you to help to develop closer relationships with your clients and see the opportunities for you to contribute to injury prevention – within your coaching guidelines.

There's movement development training, which helps you turn **any** exercise or movement into an injury prevention super move, so you can eliminate the need for dedicating time to mobility training.

There's advanced movement analysis and strength evolution training that creates lightning quick assessments so you can deliver individually targeted and hugely effective advice in seconds, even in a group setting.

There's injury impact and fallout training. This takes your coaching skills beyond anything other coaches can dream of, and easily builds trust and rapport with clients and other professionals along the way.

And there's network building training, helping you future proof your business and become a vital part of any injury management conversation or team.

LEVEL 1: The Vault of Injury Prevention Secrets

This is communication and coaching analysis training at it's very best. You'll be able to see injuries coming before your clients are even aware that there's an issue – and know exactly what you can do about it. It's your gateway to a whole new world of opportunity within your sports or fitness coaching.

Here's a summary of what this training does.

- See injuries coming before they become painful - You're going to be able to use clues from your clients' body language to decipher potential injury problems long before they become painful.

- Discover hidden opportunities - Your existing coaching structure presents so many untapped opportunities, you'll be able to surpass any previous results for your clients and raise the bar for all the other coaches out there.

- Avoid the traps – Too often coaches are drawn into traps with mobility and injury prevention, you're going to be able to identify them all and easily sidestep every single one.

- Step into your full potential – Not every coach is prepared for what they'll discover. But those who are ready – you'll be given the chance to shine.

LEVEL 2 THE SMARTT® Coach Certification

With this movement development training, we're redefining coaching standards and accelerating results.

Here's a summary of what this training does.

- Revolutionise warming up – This is by far the most overlooked and underutilised area of fitness coaching. You'll be shown how to transform yours so that your clients are more capable of the upcoming workout and preventing injury in half the time.

- Eliminate stretching - You'll discover how to keep your client safe from injury without the need for stretching or dedicated mobility training.

- Accelerate your clients' performances - Use simple tweaks in your existing coaching practices to help your clients get faster and stronger with less effort.

- Develop more income streams - maximise your new skills to expand your sources of income. Even if coaching is just a hobby.

LEVEL 3: TECHNIQUE & PERFORMANCE SPECIALIST

This truly is the Formula One of strength training & movement analysis. We'll make your coaching laser targeted and lightning quick.

Here's a summary of what this training does:

- Shatter illusions about technique problems - You'll discover three fundamental factors that underpin all the problems you see and develop the skills to deal with them fast.

- Fortify strength training principles - evolve your strength training to bulletproof your clients' movement, even under extreme load.

- Accelerate assessments - make effective assessments of your clients' movements in seconds (even online) to avoid disruption to your clients training

- Enhanced skill acquisition – fast-track the effectiveness of your clients' movement without the need for endlessly repetitive drills

- Exceed your clients' expectations - No training has ever made your coaching more efficient, targeted and individualised.

LEVEL 4: INJURY PREVENTION & RECOVERY SPECIALIST

This training is the ultimate in cohesion and multi-disciplinary medicine.

Here's a summary of what this training does:

- Complement the work of other professionals - Make it easy for other professionals to want to work alongside you.

Discover what makes them tick the results they're looking for and how you can easily help them achieve that.

- Establish yourself as a leader in your niche – Quickly become the "go to" coach in your specific area of sport or fitness when it comes to injuries.

- Ease your clients' worries – Never before has it been easier to ease your clients fears around the injury issue so they can get results faster than ever before.

- Fast-track your client's injury recovery. Take a leading role in shortening injury recovery times for your clients.

LEVEL 5: THE CHANGE MAKERS' MASTERMIND

Now you can future proof your sports coaching or fitness business.

Here's a summary of what this training does:

- Create an unstoppable stream of your dream clients – building a network of like-minded professionals clubs and other coaches will ensure your dream customers find you and are eager to work with you.

- Make you an indispensable part of the team - Your results will demonstrate your expertise so that other professionals see you as a vital part of their injury management team.

- Stay focused on the specific part of coaching you love - Creating your own unique ecosystem will ensure that you are positioned within it at your favourite point so you can concentrate on doing the things that you love best.

- Brainstorm with others - Surrounding yourself with a small group of other professionals who are trying to achieve the same as you will give you insights and shortcuts you won't find anywhere else.

BONUS: THE SMARTT® SAFE MARK

Achieve the gold standard and have your excellence recognised. The SMARTT® Safe Mark is instant recognition of your business or club's dedication to preventing injuries.

Here's a summary of what this step does:

- Become the most popular club or fitness business in town - Use the SMARTT® Safe Mark logo to demonstrate your commitment to and achievement with injury prevention within your club or business which will attract new members or clients

- Get recognised within your sport or fitness niche - achieving the SMARTT® Safe mark will demonstrate that your club or business is willing to go above and beyond for their members, which will help you achieve other accolades within the industry.

- Be the leader in your niche - When other clubs and businesses see that you have achieved this mark of excellence, they will want that too, which raises everyone's standards.

- Establish your reputation of excellence - Build instant trust with brand new clients and other professionals who want to work with you.

CASE STUDY: JUSTINE HUDSON

A painful labral tear handled easily and positively with super-fast results.

Justine's experience is just one of many that I've had the pleasure of creating over the last few years she was diagnosed with a painful labral tear on her hip

She was struggling to move without significant discomfort. She'd been to see a local therapist Martin, who was keen for her to avoid surgery and suggested the collagen injection to promote healing within the damaged tissue. The thought of an injection made her nervous, and she was desperate to do anything she could to ease the pain.

She'd seen Martin the day before, and he'd recommended that she come back in two weeks for the injection but this left Justine feeling frustrated and alone as she faced the prospect of two whole weeks without pain relief, or any kind of action plan...but this is where the SMARTT® methods shine!

One of the worst feelings for people in pain is the one of helplessness and a lack of control - and if we add that to a complete lack of understanding about the condition, the result is that our clients scour the internet for information about what they have, and what they should do. But in most cases, this doesn't actually help. In fact, it just leaves our clients feeling more confused than ever, and sometimes simply terrified that they have some kind of incurable problem.

This is exactly what happened to Justine.

So, when she asked for my help, the very first thing I did was explained to her why the tear had happened in the first place and what Martin was trying to achieve with his collagen injection.

When she felt confident that she understood what was happening in her body, I gave her a series of simple movement videos to follow that she could do every day whenever suited her...as long as all her movement was pain free.

All the movements were designed to help relieve the strain on the labrum and increase the blood flow to that area to promote healing. None of these movements caused increased strain, were painful in the slightest or tried in any way to deal directly with a painful area.

Calm confident clients take action to help themselves.

After about a week, she mentioned that her thigh didn't feel as tight and that the pain of move from a hip to an ache in a low back, which meant that she'd reduce the strain on labrum, and her back was just tired from being strained too.

But of course, experiencing this improvement gives rise to hope...and hope leads to more frustrations when you still can't do what you normally would, which leads to more questions.

The problem is that most therapists don't have a facility for clients to ask questions when they have them, so clients end up having to wait until the next appointment. But fitness coaches have great communication channels with their clients. And that's why Justine felt comfortable pinging me a message about her frustrations.

Within a few hours, she had answers to her questions, which meant that she was sticking to the programming and confident that she was helping her own situation, rather than worrying that she would hurt herself further, which usually means not doing anything, or doing too much (and hurting herself further) because she didn't understand what was happening.

Just by my being part of the team dealing with this problem, Justine felt supported and was making progress. And this in itself made a massive difference to her during the stressful and daunting time in her life. But be under no illusions, in situations like this _movement alone is not enough_ to cure the problem.

But then neither was Martin's approach. An injection by itself might have helped ease the pain for a little while. But it wouldn't have done anything to remove the major contributing factors to the tear happening in the first place, which means it could easily and would be very likely to happen again.

And that's why working together in complimentary, yet completely different capacities, is the best way to get the fastest results.

Small changes make big lives in your big differences in your clients lives yet all changes can be measured...and that's okay.

Instead of waiting two weeks in agony with no way of making progress, Justine was able to take immediate and positive action, which reduced her pain and put her mind at ease.

Because of that action at the end of the two weeks her situation could have improved enough for Martin to decide on a different treatment path for the changes in the symptoms that she presented. It could have helped the injection be more effective. It could have shortened her recovery by weeks, if not months.

While it's impossible to know the future, we do know this: that without the SMARTT® methods, Justine would have spent two weeks worried in pain and feeling very alone.

And the craziest thing of all is that I've never met Martin or had any contact with him about this issue. yet I can still support his treatment approach to give Justine the best possible outcome, which is what we all want!

Of course, problems like this don't magically disappear overnight. And Justine's situation is ongoing. But we are working together to ensure that this issue and many others associated with the underlying causes of it don't happen again.

✻ ✻ ✻

REVEALED! THE TRUE POWER OF INJURY PREVENTION

This is how fitness coaches become real superheroes. When the ripples of our small actions are felt by everyone, you can help change the world. The framework I've outlined in this book will help you to build stronger connections with your immediate clients, help them to avoid injury and to establish yourself as a leader in the industry. But the benefits don't stop there. By working together, every fitness coach across the world can be part of a much bigger story that can have a positive impact on everyone. You see, injuries don't just affect our individual clients, they're devastating healthcare systems, businesses and entire economies too. But we have the power to change that!

For every individual that we help avoid pain. We're saving healthcare systems, the cost of appointments, medications, specialists, equipment, and all the unseen costs that accumulate as a person's pain gets worse, more prolonged and more debilitating.

We're saving companies from the loss in productivity and the rising cost of sick days, which has a direct impact on our economies. And we're saving generations of older people the devastating blow of losing their independence as they're forced to move out of their home into a care facility.

By following this framework, I've been proving for years that most non collision injuries are completely avoidable, yet it's these small aches and pains that seem to appear out of nowhere that are costing our society the most. It's the tight hamstring that develops into a tear that later develops into knee pain that develops eventually into osteoarthritis and requires major surgery.

Musculoskeletal like injuries like these affect every group of our society, they prevent young athletes from following their dreams. They cause working age adults to lose out financially if they have to miss work, and they strip our elderly population of their independence. But regardless of the age of the person suffering, chronic pain increases feelings of anxiety and depression, which can eventually lead to isolation, loneliness, and even addiction to prescription medication.

Not to mention the inability to exercise which cycles them back to the risk of developing all the lifestyle diseases they were trying to avoid in the first place.

It's time for every coach to show the world what we made of. While everyone else is waiting, we're taking ACTION!

As a society, we've ended up in this mess because we've been waiting for the pain to come before taking action.

But most sports and fitness coaches know that our clients don't need to be in pain for these problems to affect their ability to exercise. Even the fear of irritating previous pain is enough to destroy motivation and consistency of training.

Waiting for the pain means that we're missing the opportunity to prevent these problems. And that's how you can help change the world and show the industry just what can be achieved if we take a more proactive, collaborative approach. By playing your part and actively trying to prevent these injuries, you'll become part of a collective. And it's this collective that has the power to change the world.

Your individual efforts are like throwing a small pebble into a big pond, it will make small ripples. But our collective contribution is like hurtling a meteor into the ocean, it'll create a tidal wave.

It has always been my vision to make sporting injuries across the world, the exception rather than the rule and by everyone working together using the SMARTT® methods, we can actually make it happen. And that means happier, healthier populations who live in societies that don't have to bear the financial and emotional cost of chronic pain.

This means that more money can be spent on schools, hospitals, transport, the environment, opportunities and all the other topics that we care so passionately about. So, I guess the question now is, are you ready to join us?

The 5 Steps of Injury Prevention

So how did I do? Do you understand the five steps presented in this guide?

Step 1: Breaking the Barriers – Understanding the power of non-verbal communication, recognising the signs and knowing what to do about them

Step 2: Activating Stealth Mode – Making it easy for your clients to do the things they don't like doing (and have fun while they're at it!)

Step 3: Building Your Superpowers – Making lightning-fast assessments and creating robust and resilient clients

Step 4: Connecting the Dots – Recognising your vital role in the injury conversation and learning how your skills complement other therapies

Step 5: Becoming Indispensable – Creating your own ecosystem of other coaches and professionals to secure the future of your business/club

You don't have to know how to put these steps into practice right now, but do you understand the benefits of each step?

※ ※ ※

A PERSONAL MESSAGE FROM SARAH J. PITTS

Well, there you go. I hope you are blown away with the potential that has been presented to you in this guide. If you are, then I highly encourage you to get involved with our community at injuryhackers.com. There is no doubt in my mind that this is the solution for you.

On the other hand, you could be feeling a little overwhelmed. You might feel like you're drowning in possibilities if you made it this far, and that's okay. Remember, you don't have to understand everything that was presented in this guide right this second. It took me years to master what was presented here.

The reason I revealed the five steps to you was to get you excited about the **possibilities open to you**. I wanted you to understand that I actually have the answer to your problems. I've devoted the last five years of my life to creating the training strategies and resources that I've mentioned in this guide, but you're able to take it as far as you'd like. At least you now know that you have a roadmap to follow (see more at mostmotion.com/roadmap). You know exactly what you can be working towards, and you know where to find the solution.

I call this entire process "Injury Hacking" because we're breaking injury problems down into small pieces that makes helping out more accessible to more coaches. We're finding ways of everyone being able to get involved and contributing to the ultimate goal of eliminating sporting injuries for good.

If you like what you've read in this book and you'd like to meet other like-minded sports and fitness coaches from around the world, then I'd like to invite you to join our Facebook group at http://injuryhackers.com . Enjoy.

❊ ❊ ❊

See the 5 Steps in Action With...

"The Injury Hacker's Solution to Knee Pain"

This FREE Breakthrough Framework Training Reveals The Greatest Goldmine of Knee Pain Secrets Ever Crammed Into A Simple Plan!

Grab your copy NOW!

https://mostmotion.com/injuryhackerkneepain

FREE Online Training Will Show You The Secrets You Need to Help Clients Avoid The Same Knee Pain Struggles You've Had.

* * *

Printed in Great Britain
by Amazon